PATRICIA LAUBER

VOLCANO

The Eruption and Healing of Mount St. Helens

BRADBURY PRESS • NEW YORK

ACKNOWLEDGMENTS

The author is greatly indebted to the scientists and naturalists who helped with her research by giving generously of their time and special knowledge. Some were also kind enough to read and comment on the manuscript. In particular she would like to thank:

At United States Forest Service, Dr. Joseph E. Means, research forester, Dr. James E. Sedell, aquatic ecologist, and Dr. Frederick J. Swanson, research geologist, Pacific Northwest Forest and Range Experiment Station, Forest Sciences Laboratory, Corvallis, Oregon; James M. Gale, chief naturalist, and Jim Quiring, Mount St. Helens National Volcanic Monument.

At United States Geological Survey, Dr. Donald W. Peterson and Dr. Kenneth McGee, David A. Johnston Cascades Volcano Observatory, Vancouver, Washington.

At Oregon State University, College of Forestry, Dr. Gary Hunt.

Some of the above were also most helpful when it came to assembling the photographs for this book, as were Bernie Pineda, Mount St. Helens National Volcanic Monument, and Dr. Douglas C. Andersen, Department of Forestry and Natural Resources, Purdue University.

The author would also like to thank Thom Corcoran, Public Affairs, Gifford Pinchot National Forest, Jim Hughes, photographer, Office of Information, Pacific Northwest Region, USDA Forest Service, and Lyn Topinka, photographer, David A. Johnston Cascades Volcano Observatory, for help generously given.

ILLUSTRATION CREDITS

Douglas C. Andersen, Purdue University, while conducting research sponsored by the National Science Foundation: pp. 40 (bottom), 41. Sylvia Frezzolini: p. 53. Patricia Lauber: pp. 11 (top), 49 (bottom). Ralph Perry/Black Star: p. 26. ©Gary Rosenquist/EARTH IMAGES: pp. 7 (top), 8. USDA Forest Service: pp. 2 (left), 11 (bottom), 24, 28 (top left, bottom right), 29, 42, 43, 44, 46 (bottom), 48 (bottom), 52, 55; photos by James M. Gale: pp. 30 (top), 32 (bottom), 36 (bottom left), 57; photos by Jim Hughes: title page, pp. iv, 17 (bottom), 31, 38, 49 (top, center); photo by Stephen Nofield: p. 33; photos from Gifford Pinchot National Forest: pp. 3, 36 (top left); photos by Bernie Pineda: pp. 28 (top right), 40 (top), 47, 54; photos by Jim Quiring: pp. 30 (bottom), 32 (top), 34, 35, 36 (top right, bottom right), 37 (top, bottom right), 45, 48 (top); photos by Chuck Tonn: p. 19; photo by Francisco Valenzuela: p. 56. United States Department of the Interior, U.S. Geological Survey, David A. Johnston Cascades Volcano Observatory, Vancouver, Washington: pp. 2 (right), 7 (bottom), 23 (bottom); photo by Philip J. Carpenter: p. 17 (top); photo by Tom Casadevall: p. 15; photos by Harry Glicken: pp. 5 (right), 6, 18; photos by Terry Leighley: pp. 14 (right), 21; photo by Peter W. Lipman: p. 14 (left); photo by Austin Post: p. 13; photos by Donald A. Swanson: pp. 4, 5 (left); photos by Lyn Topinka: pp. 10, 12, 16, 17 (center), 20, 22, 23 (top), 37 (bottom left), 46 (top), 50, 58, and jacket.

Cover: Mount St. Helens as it appeared two years after the big eruption of May 18, 1980. The volcano was giving off gas and ash. At the center of the big new crater was a dome that grew as eruptions added thick, pasty lava to it.

Title page: The May 18, 1980, eruption tore the top off Mount St. Helens, leaving a horseshoe-shaped crater. Here St. Helens is seen from above the clouds, with Mount Adams, another volcano in the Cascade Range, in the background.

10 9 8 7 6 5 4 3

The text of this book is set in 14 point Baskerville. Book design by Sylvia Frezzolini

Library of Congress Cataloging-in-Publication Data
Lauber, Patricia. Volcano : the eruption and healing of Mount St. Helens.
Summary: An account of how and why Mount St. Helens erupted in May 1980 and the destruction it caused, and a discussion of the return of life to that area. 1. Saint Helens, Mount (Wash.)—Eruption, 1980—Juvenile literature. [1. Saint Helens, Mount (Wash.)—Eruption, 1980. 2. Volcanoes] I. Title. QE523.S23L38 1986   551.2′1′0979784   85-22442   ISBN 0-02-754500-8

Contents

Mount St. Helens, in southern Washington State, was long considered one of the most beautiful mountains in the Cascade Range, with its gleaming snow-capped peak that formed an almost perfect cone. This photograph, taken in 1972, shows Spirit Lake in the foreground.

ONE

The Volcano Wakes

For many years the volcano slept. It was silent and still, big and beautiful. Then the volcano, which was named Mount St. Helens, began to stir. On March 20, 1980, it was shaken by a strong earthquake. The quake was a sign of movement inside St. Helens. It was a sign of a waking volcano that might soon erupt again.

Mount St. Helens was built by many eruptions over thousands of years. In each eruption hot rock from inside the earth forced its way to the surface. The rock was so hot that it was molten, or melted, and it had gases trapped in it. The name for such rock is magma. Once the molten rock reaches the surface it is called lava. In some eruptions the magma was fairly liquid. Its gases escaped gently. Lava flowed out of the volcano, cooled, and hardened. In other eruptions the magma was thick and sticky. Its gases burst out violently, carrying along sprays of molten rock. As it blasted into the sky, the rock cooled and hardened. Some of it rained down as ash—tiny bits of rock. Some rained down as pumice—frothy rock puffed up by gases.

Together the lava flows, ash, and pumice built a mountain with a bowl-shaped crater at its top. St. Helens grew to a height of 9,677 feet, so high that its peak was often hidden by clouds. Its big neighbors were built in the same way. Mount St. Helens is part of the Cascade Range, a chain

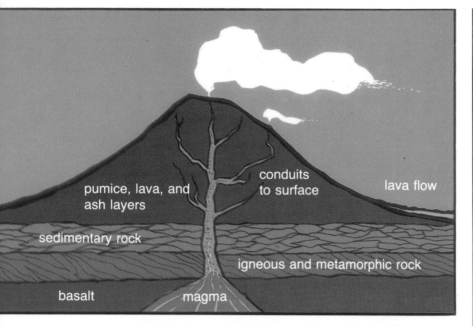

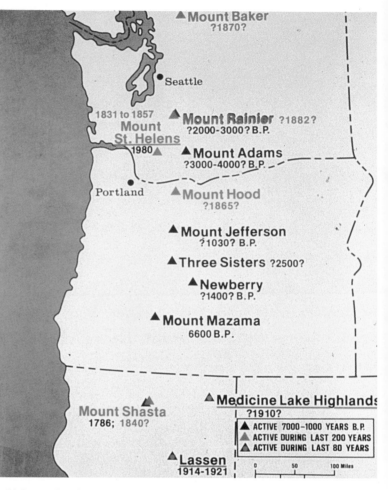

A volcano is a place where hot, molten rock from inside the earth comes to the surface. Mount St. Helens was built by many eruptions over thousands of years.

Map shows the Cascade Range in the United States and the periods in which each volcano last erupted. Question marks mean that the dates are not certain. The letters *B.P.* stand for *before present*.

of volcanoes that runs from northern California into British Columbia.

In the middle 1800s a number of small eruptions took place. Between 1832 and 1857 St. Helens puffed out clouds of steam and ash from time to time. It also gave off small flows of lava. Then the mountain fell still.

For well over a hundred years the volcano slept. Each spring, as winter snows melted, its slopes seemed to come alive. Wildflowers bloomed in meadows. Bees gathered pollen and nectar. Birds fed, found mates, and built nests. Bears lumbered out of their dens. Herds of elk and deer feasted on fresh green shoots. Thousands of people came to hike, picnic, camp, fish, paint, bird-watch, or just enjoy the scenery. Logging crews felled tall trees and planted seedlings.

2

These people knew that Mount St. Helens was a volcano, but they did not fear it. To them it was simply a green and pleasant mountain, where forests of firs stretched up the slopes and streams ran clear and cold.

Visitors enjoyed the sight of wild animals, forested slopes, and clear cold waters.

The mountain did not seem so trustworthy to geologists, scientists who study the earth. They knew that Mount St. Helens was dangerous. It was a young volcano and one of the most active in the Cascade Range. In 1975 two geologists finished a study of the volcano's past eruptions. They predicted that Mount St. Helens would erupt again within 100 years, perhaps before the year 2000.

The geologists were right. With the earthquake of March 20, 1980, Mount St. Helens woke from a sleep of 123 years. Magma had forced its way into the mountain, tearing apart solid rock. The snapping of that rock set off the shock waves that shook St. Helens. That quake was followed by many others. Most of them were smaller, but they came so fast and so often that it was hard to tell when one quake ended and another began.

On March 27 people near Mount St. Helens heard a tremendous explosion. The volcano began to blow out steam and ash that stained its

Ash darkened the mountain's gleaming peak.

snow-white peak. Small explosions went on into late April, stopped, started again on May 7, and stopped on May 14.

The explosions of late March opened up two new craters at the top of the mountain. One formed inside the old crater. The other formed nearby. The two new craters grew bigger. Soon they joined, forming one large crater that continued to grow during the next few weeks. Meanwhile, the north face of the mountaintop was swelling and cracking. The swelling formed a bulge that grew outward at a rate of five to six feet a day.

Geologists were hard at work on the waking volcano. They took samples of ash and gases, hoping to find clues to what was happening inside. They placed instruments on the mountain to record earthquakes and the tilting of ground. They kept measuring the bulge. A sudden change in its rate of growth might be a sign that the volcano was about to erupt. But the bulge grew steadily, and the ash and gases yielded no clues.

Measurements with a surveyor's level were made to see if the ground was tilting, a sign of rising magma.

When the weather was clear, geologists could monitor the bulge from various bases, such as Coldwater II. On May 17 this geologist, Harry Glicken, was joined by another, David Johnston.

Glicken and Johnston visited the bulge by helicopter. Johnston took gas samples. Later, Glicken went off duty and Johnston took over at Coldwater II. The next morning he was killed by the eruption.

By mid-May the bulge was huge. Half a mile wide and more than a mile long, it had swelled out 300 feet.

On Sunday morning, May 18, the sun inched up behind the Cascades, turning the sky pink. By 8 a.m. the sun was above the mountains, the sky blue, the air cool. There was not one hint of what was to come.

At 8:32 Mount St. Helens erupted. Billowing clouds of smoke, steam, and ash hid the mountain from view and darkened the sky for miles.

The eruption went on until evening. By its end a fan-shaped area of destruction stretched out to the north, covering some 230 square miles. Within that area 57 people and countless plants and animals had died.

Geologists now faced two big jobs. One was to keep watch on the mountain, to find out if more eruptions were building up. If so, they hoped to learn how to predict the eruptions.

The other job was to find out exactly what had happened on May 18. Most volcanic eruptions start slowly. Why had Mount St. Helens erupted suddenly? What events had caused the big fan-shaped area of destruction? What had become of the mountaintop, which was now 1,200 feet lower?

The mountain disappeared in billowing clouds of hot gas, ash, and rock.

The answers to these questions came slowly as geologists studied instrument records and photographs, interviewed witnesses, and studied the clues left by the eruption itself. But in time they pieced together a story that surprised them. This eruption turned out to be very different from the ones that built Mount St. Helens.

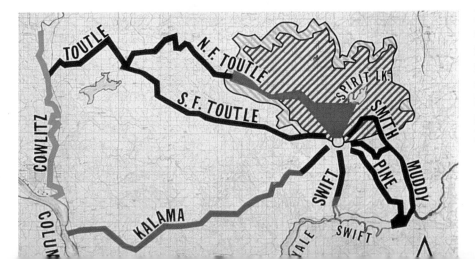

Red stripes mark the area of destruction caused by the blast. Yellow stripes mark the area where trees were left standing but were killed by heat. Solid red shows the avalanche path.

At 8:32 on the morning of May 18, 1980, an earthquake triggered an avalanche that tore open the volcano and unleashed a searing blast of steam and rock.

TWO

The Big Blast

The May 18 eruption began with an earthquake that triggered an avalanche. At 8:32 a.m. instruments that were miles away registered a strong earthquake. The pilot and passengers of a small plane saw the north side of the mountain rippling and churning. Shaken by the quake, the bulge was tearing loose. It began to slide, in a huge avalanche that carried along rock ripped from deep inside Mount St. Helens.

The avalanche tore open the mountain. A scalding blast shot sideways out of the opening. It was a blast of steam, from water heated by rising magma.

Normally water cannot be heated beyond its boiling point, which is 212 degrees Fahrenheit at sea level. At boiling point, water turns to a gas, which we call steam. But if water is kept under pressure, it can be heated far beyond its boiling point and still stay liquid. (That is how a pressure cooker works.) If the pressure is removed, this superheated water suddenly turns, or flashes, to steam. As steam it takes up much more room—it expands. The sudden change to steam can cause an explosion.

Before the eruption Mount St. Helens was like a giant pressure cooker. The rock inside it held superheated water. The water stayed liquid because it was under great pressure, sealed in the mountain. When the mountain was torn open, the pressure was suddenly relieved. The super-heated water flashed to steam. Expanding violently, it shattered rock inside the mountain and exploded out the opening, traveling at speeds of up to 200 miles an hour.

The blast flattened whole forests of 180-foot-high firs. It snapped off or uprooted the trees, scattering the trunks as if they were straws. At first, this damage was puzzling. A wind of 200 miles an hour is not strong enough to level forests of giant trees. The explanation, geologists later discovered, was that the wind carried rocks ranging in size from grains of sand to blocks as big as cars. As the blast roared out of the volcano, it swept up and carried along the rock it had shattered.

The result was what one geologist described as "a stone wind." It was a wind of steam and rocks, traveling at high speed. The rocks gave the blast its great force. Before it, trees snapped and fell. Their stumps looked as if they had been sandblasted. The wind of stone rushed on. It stripped bark and branches from trees and uprooted them, leveling 150 square miles of countryside. At the edge of this area other trees were left standing, but the heat of the blast scorched and killed them.

The blast leveled whole forests of huge firs. The tiny figures of two scientists (lower right) give an idea of scale.

Shredded stumps looked as if they had been sandblasted.

Outside the blast zone, surviving trees were covered with ash that lasted for months.

The stone wind was traveling so fast that it overtook and passed the avalanche. On its path was Spirit Lake, one of the most beautiful lakes in the Cascades. The blast stripped the trees from the slopes surrounding the lake and moved on.

Meanwhile the avalanche had hit a ridge and split. One part of it poured into Spirit Lake, adding a 180-foot layer of rock and dirt to the bottom of the lake. The slide of avalanche into the lake forced the water out. The water sloshed up the slopes, then fell back into the lake. With it came thousands of trees felled by the blast.

The main part of the avalanche swept down the valley of the North Fork of the Toutle River. There, in the valley, most of the avalanche slowed and stopped. It covered 24 square miles and averaged 150 feet thick.

The blast itself continued for 10 to 15 minutes, then stopped. Minutes later Mount St. Helens began to erupt upwards. A dark column of ash and ground-up rock rose miles into the sky. Winds blew the ash eastward. Lightning flashed in the ash cloud and started forest fires. In Yakima, Washington, some 80 miles away, the sky turned so dark that street lights

Material from the avalanche that poured into Spirit Lake can be seen in the foreground of this photograph. Some of the trees that washed into the lake can be seen on its far side. Mount Rainier, another Cascade volcano, is in the background.

A gigantic column of ash and gas rose miles into the sky.

went on at noon. Ash fell like snow that would not melt. This eruption continued for nine hours.

Shortly after noon the color of the ash column changed. It became lighter, a sign that the volcano was now throwing out mostly new magma. Until then much of the ash had been made of old rock.

At the same time the volcano began giving off huge flows of pumice and ash. The material was very hot, with temperatures of about 1,000 degrees Fahrenheit, and it traveled down the mountain at speeds of 100 miles an hour. The flows went on until 5:30 in the afternoon. They formed a wedge-shaped plain of pumice on the side of the mountain. Two weeks later temperatures in the pumice were still 780 degrees.

Hot flows of pumice and ash also occurred during smaller eruptions of the summer and fall of 1980.

An eruption on March 19, 1982, melted snow and caused this mudflow. The smaller part of the flow went into Spirit Lake (lower left), while the larger part traveled down the Toutle River.

Finally, there were the mudflows, which started when heat from the blast melted ice and snow on the mountaintop. The water mixed with ash, pumice, ground-up rock, and dirt and rocks of the avalanche. The result was a thick mixture that was like wet concrete, a mudflow. The mudflows traveled fast, scouring the landscape and sweeping down the slopes into river valleys. Together their speed and thickness did great damage.

The largest mudflow was made of avalanche material from the valley of the North Fork of the Toutle River. It churned down the river valley, tearing out steel bridges, ripping houses apart, picking up boulders and

15

The depth of the May 18, 1980, mudflow can be seen in the traces it left on trees along the Muddy River.

trucks and carrying them along. Miles away it choked the Cowlitz River and blocked shipping channels in the Columbia River.

When the sun rose on May 19, it showed a greatly changed St. Helens. The mountain was 1,200 feet shorter than it had been the morning before. Most of the old top had slid down the mountain in the avalanche. The rest had erupted out as shattered rock. Geologists later figured that the volcano had lost three quarters of a cubic mile of old rock.

The north side of the mountain had changed from a green and lovely slope to a fan-shaped wasteland.

At the top of Mount St. Helens was a big, new crater with the shape of a horseshoe. Inside the crater was the vent, the opening through which rock and gases erupted from time to time over the next few years.

16

The mudflow roared through a logging camp, overturning large pieces of equipment.

It swept up and carried along huge boulders and tore out bridges.

On May 17, 1980, Mount St. Helens, as seen from Coldwater II, had a soaring, ash-stained peak and green forests climbing its slopes. The next day the big eruption tore the top off the mountain and flattened the forests, as shown in the September 9, 1980, photograph taken from the same place at Coldwater II.

Boot Lake before and after the eruption.

By May 1983 the dome was huge. Note the size of the two scientists (lower left) standing on the crater floor beside the dome.

In 1980 St. Helens erupted six more times. Most of these eruptions were explosive—ash soared into the air, pumice swept down the north side of the mountain. In the eruptions of June and August, thick pasty lava oozed out of the vent and built a dome. But both domes were

20

destroyed by the next eruptions. In October the pattern changed. The explosions stopped, and thick lava built a dome that was not destroyed. Later eruptions added to the dome, making it bigger and bigger.

Crack in dome shows red-hot molten rock just below the surface.

During this time, geologists were learning to read the clues found before eruptions. They learned to predict what St. Helens was going to do. The predictions helped to protect people who were on and near the mountain.

To learn what the volcano may do, scientists make many kinds of measurements, trying to follow the movements of magma inside Mount St. Helens. Many are made inside the crater. In this photograph, scientists can be seen lower left. The dome is to the right, the crater wall to the left.

With his instruments shielded from the sun, this geologist is measuring the dome. Swelling may be a sign an eruption is building up.

When magma moves, it causes earthquakes. These scientists are installing a seismometer, which senses earthquakes.

Scientists also sample the gases given off by magma. A sharp increase in sulfur dioxide often tells of a coming eruption.

In 1982 Congress set aside 110,000 acres around the volcano as the Mount St. Helens National Volcanic Monument. Outside the monument, bulldozers could clean up and forests be replanted. Inside the monument little was to be changed so that scientists could study what had happened and was happening at Mount St. Helens, and so that visitors of all ages could see the effects of the eruption and the return of life.

Among these people were many natural scientists. They had come to look for survivors, for plants and animals that had lived through the eruption. They had come to look for colonizers, for plants and animals that would move in. Mount St. Helens had erupted many times before. Each time life had returned. Now scientists would have a chance to see how it did. They would see how nature healed itself.

After the big eruption, the north slope of Mount St. Helens looked like the surface of the moon. Searchers from the helicopter looked in vain for human survivors here.

THREE

Survivors and Colonizers

In early summer of 1980 the north side of Mount St. Helens looked like the surface of the moon—gray and lifeless. The slopes were buried under mud, ground-up rock, pumice, and bits of trees. Ash covered everything with a thick crust. The eruption had set off thunderstorms that wet the falling ash. The ash became goo that hardened into a crust. The slopes looked like a place where nothing could be alive or ever live again. Yet life was there.

With the coming of warm weather, touches of green appeared among the grays and browns. They were the green of plants that had survived the force and heat of the eruption.

Some plants had still been buried under the snows of winter on May 18. Huckleberry and trillium sprang up among the fallen forest trees. So did young silver firs and mountain hemlocks.

In other places, where the snow had melted, the blast swept away the parts of plants that were aboveground. But roots, bulbs, and stems remained alive underground. They sprouted, and hardy shoots pushed up through the pumice and ash. Among these was fireweed, one of the first plants to appear after a fire.

A few plants were even growing in blocks of soil that had been lifted from one place and dropped in another.

Trillium grew and flowered.

Huckleberry plants grew
in stump soil.

Plants from the forest floor
sprouted on the root wad of
a fallen tree.

Sedge grew through the
crust of ash.

Fireweed appeared through
cracks in the ash.

Ground squirrels were other underground survivors.

Some small animals had also survived under the snowpack or below ground. There were chipmunks, white-footed deer mice, and red squirrels. There were pocket gophers, small rodents that carry food in fur-lined pockets in their cheeks.

Ants survived underground. So did eggs laid by insects. Many other small animals, such as springtails and mites, lived through the eruption in their homes of rotting logs.

Snow and ice still covered a few lakes on May 18. Here fish, frogs, salamanders, crayfish, snakes, and water insects were alive on May 19.

Termites survived in rotting logs.

Meta Lake, here shown in 1984, was protected by a cover of mushy snow and ice at the time of the blast. Its frogs, crayfish, and other animals were survivors.

Natural scientists also found many tiny living things. They found more kinds of bacteria than they could name. They found fungi, which are very simple plants. Fungi lack the green coloring matter called chlorophyll and cannot make their own food, as green plants do. They take their nourishment from other living things or from once-living things, like rotten wood. Fungi can reproduce in several ways. One is by making spores, which are as small as specks of dust. Fungus spores are everywhere. When conditions are right for them, they sprout and grow. In the summer of 1980 scientists at Mount St. Helens saw fire fungi, which often appear after forest fires. Their spores need great heat to sprout.

31

Both fungus spores and bacteria are very light, and they can travel thousands of miles on the wind. So no one could really tell which were survivors and which were colonizers. But even in that first summer, scientists could see many other colonizers arriving.

The earliest came by air. Light seeds of willow and cottonwood blew in. Insects blew or flew in. And then there were the spiders, which ballooned in. Many kinds of young spiders spin threads of silk that remain attached to their bodies. When the wind catches these threads, it lifts the spiders into the air and carries them for miles.

Willow seeds travel on wind-borne clouds of silky fluff.

Young spiders balloon in.

The scientists also saw animal visitors. Birds flew in. Coyotes, elk, deer, and other large mammals passed through, perhaps looking for food and water.

This herd of elk is passing through a mudflow area.

That first summer there were not many plants and animals on the north slope. But there was a wide variety. So natural scientists were able to start studying the links among these forms of life, for no living thing exists all by itself. Each is linked to other living things and to its surroundings. All need food and places to live.

Scientists knew, for example, that over a year or so the crust of ash would break up and wash away. But they saw important small changes taking place in the summer of 1980. There were areas where snow lay under the ash. When the warmth of summer melted the snow, it no longer supported the ash. The ash slumped and broke up. Here surviving roots could send up shoots. Heavy rains sent water running down the slopes. The water cut channels in the ash. Here, too, roots could send up shoots.

Huckleberry plants thrive in a channel cut by running water.

Deer and elk wandered through. They fed on some of the plants. But their sharp hooves broke up more of the ash. Like other animal visitors, they brought in seeds. Some seeds had stuck in their coats. Others were in their droppings.

Hoofprints and broken ash made places that trapped seeds. They made places where seeds could sprout and get their roots into soil. They made places where plants could grow.

Hoofprints made hollows that trapped seeds and offered a place where seeds could sprout and plants could grow.

In time these plants would form seeds. The seeds would colonize other places. And every plant that grew would help still other forms of life.

Many times scientists did not actually see the animals but saw tracks or other signs of them.

They saw coyote tracks . . .

the tunnels of meadow voles . . .

deer tracks . . .

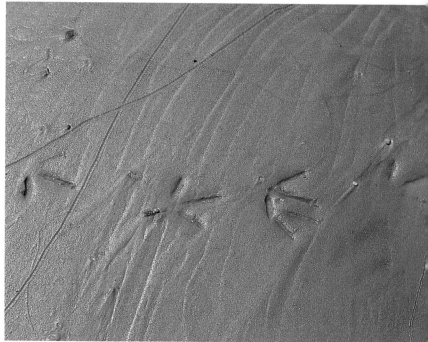

and killdeer tracks, among others.

They saw a Pacific silver fir, a survivor, stripped of bark—a sign of a porcupine.

They saw the tracks of a bear that had been eating huckleberries and then . . .

wandered up the mountain, perhaps looking for more food. There was none. But the bear left droppings that held huckleberries and their seeds. New plants may have grown from those seeds.

In the summer of 1980 a few hardy plants, like this lupine, provided food and shelter to insects and spiders. It was an island of life in the gray wilderness.

FOUR

Links and More Links

Here and there in the gray wilderness, a hardy plant grew—perhaps fireweed or lupine. It seemed to be the only living thing around, but it wasn't. Beneath its leaves were ants, ladybugs, aphids, grasshoppers, beetles, spiders, and other small animals. The plant was an island of life, an island of survivors and colonizers.

Each kind of life made some other kind possible. The aphids, for example, sucked sap from the plant. Ants fed on the sweet honeydew that aphids give off. Ladybugs ate aphids. Spiders trapped and ate insects and also other spiders.

Some meadows and areas of clear-cut forests had groups of plant survivors. With them were animal survivors, white-footed deer mice and pocket gophers. Insects and spiders had arrived as colonizers. The mice ate seeds and insects. The gophers ate roots and bulbs, but they also did something that helped plants.

Gophers spend much of their time tunneling. They dig tunnels as they search for food underground. They dig other tunnels to live in. When digging, a gopher spreads its hind feet wide apart. It digs with its big front feet and claws, sending the loosened dirt back under its body. The dirt piles up behind it. From time to time the gopher turns and pushes the dirt back along the tunnel. At the mouth of the tunnel it gives a big shove and flings the dirt out onto the surface.

By looking under the leaves of plants, naturalists could learn what small animals were living there.

At the mouth of its tunnel a pocket gopher shoves out a pile of loosened dirt.

These habits make the gopher a pest in a garden. The gopher eats bulbs and roots of plants that people want. It throws out piles of dirt on the lawn. But to natural scientists at Mount St. Helens the pocket gopher was a small hero.

There gophers were tunneling in soil that was now covered with ash and pumice. By shoving soil out of their tunnels they brought it to the surface. The piles of soil became places where seeds could put down roots and plants could grow.

The roots of pearly everlasting and fireweed (above) attracted a gopher, which, in its burrowing, brought up soil.

A gopher mound, like the one seen lower right, may serve as a place where seeds can put down roots and plants can grow.

The soil itself held some seeds. And it held the spores of certain fungi. These are fungi that grow into the roots of plants. Together the fungi and the roots form a partnership. The fungi take water and mineral from the soil and pass them on to the roots. They do this job much better than roots alone can. In turn the fungi, which cannot make their own food, take sugars from the plant.

The gophers brought both soil and fungus spores to the surface. The spores sprouted. And the fungi formed partnerships with the roots of plants that grew in the soil.

When the plants grew well, their roots served as food for the gophers. Aboveground, the plants became islands of life, places where many small animals could live. The seeds of these plants spread and started still more islands of life.

Some ants found food in islands of life. Other ants had survived in places where there were no islands. They may have had some food stored underground. But to go on surviving, they needed to find food aboveground. For many ants that food turned out to be fire fungi. The fungi formed huge mats of tangled threads. Some of the mats lasted only a short time. Others grew in places where there was water and also food —bits of wood or other dead matter. These mats lasted for months. They were the only food that ants crawling over the pumice and ash could find. When ants from different colonies met at the mats, scientists saw them fight one another for the food.

The fungus mats also served as seedbeds for other plants. By the summer of 1981, the fire fungi were gone and mosses were growing in their place. The mosses, in turn, trapped seeds on their rough surfaces. The seeds sprouted and grew into green plants.

Green plants are the only living things that can make their own food. So nearly all other forms of life depend on green plants for food. Some take food from the plants. Others eat the eaters of plants.

In making their food, green plants take minerals from the soil. In nature the minerals never get used up because they are recycled. They

Fire fungi put out threadlike parts that formed mats. The mats served as food for ants and as seedbeds for other plants.

go back into the soil after animals or plants or parts of plants die. Some of the minerals may be washed out of dead material by rain or melting snow. Most are released as the dead material rots, or decays. Decay is caused by many small forms of life, such as bacteria, fungi, mites, springtails, beetles, millipedes. Some feed on dead material. Some eat bacteria and fungi but must eat the dead material to get them. Either way, the dead material is broken down and minerals go back into the soil.

On the north side of Mount St. Helens, these small forms of life broke down the remains of animals and plants killed in the eruption. They broke down the droppings of animals. They broke down leaves and stems when plants died back in autumn. Minerals were released and used in new plant growth.

A fallen maple is sending up new trees. In time the trunk will decay and enrich the soil.

Even the bodies of insects helped plants to grow. Many adult insects have short lives of only days or weeks. Also, as insects grow, they shed their hard outside covering—they molt. On the surface of ash and pumice, scientists could see the molts and dead bodies of insects. They could collect and measure them. They were surprised at the amount of carbon and other minerals in the molts and bodies. They realized that insect bodies have always enriched soil, but as one scientist said, "We never even noticed them before, because they're so small."

Insects and other small animals were food for the first birds that returned. Natural scientists think that all the birds on the north side of Mount St. Helens were killed on the morning of May 18. Later that summer there were many bird visitors, but at first only a few kinds of birds could live and breed in the area. Juncos could because they eat insects and make their nests in hollows in the ground. Woodpeckers also found food, and some found dead or broken-off trees in which they could make nest holes.

These are the eggs of a killdeer, one of the ground-nesting birds that were able to live and breed in the blast area.

Bluebirds were able to find holes in fallen trees for nests. This one is carrying nesting material.

Once woodpeckers have raised their young, they desert the nest holes. Deserted woodpecker holes helped mountain bluebirds to return. Bluebirds also nest in holes, but they cannot make their own. They must find holes that have formed naturally or that have been made by other animals.

Insects are also food for many kinds of fish. Most of these insects spend much of their lives in water. When they hatch from eggs, they do not look like their parents. They go through several stages before they turn into adults. Some, such as mayflies and caddis flies, spend most of their lives going through these stages. The adults live only long enough to mate and lay eggs.

Both fish and water insects need oxygen. In many lakes there was little oxygen during the first few years after the eruption. They were filled with trees and bits of plants. Billions upon billions of bacteria and other

45

April 1981: Dead trees cover the ground and float in Spirit Lake. A dome has grown in the crater of Mount St. Helens.

A scientist scrambles to collect water samples and learn what kinds of life are in Ryan Lake.

tiny living things were in the lakes, feeding on these materials and on one another and using up the oxygen. Surviving fish had to live near the surface, where winds stirred the water and added oxygen to it. They did not find much to eat.

That first summer there were two main insect foods for fish. One was the rat-tailed maggot, a young form of horsefly. The tail of this maggot is like a straw, and it serves as a breathing tube. In water with little oxygen, the maggot puts up its rat tail and takes oxygen from the air. The second food was the young of mosquitoes, which also have breathing tubes.

The May 18 eruption wiped out most large forms of life on the north side of Mount St. Helens. The healing of the slopes started with many small forms—bacteria, fungi, hardy weeds and seeds, insects, spiders, pocket gophers. Linked together, they formed a base that made possible the return of other kinds of life.

In 1980 a wind-blown lupine seed lodged in pumice, sprouted, and put down roots. As the plant grew, it became an island of life. Its flowers produced seeds, which blew away on the wind.

In later summers, wind-blown seeds produced whole colonies of lupine and pearly everlasting.

By the end of the first summer, some survivors had died but others were still alive and well. Colonizers had been arriving steadily. Looking up in autumn, scientists saw the air was silver with seeds and insects blowing in with the wind. Life was coming back to the volcano as it had many times before.

48

Fireweed sprouted through the ash . . .

and developed flowers, which produced seeds that blew away on their silvery fluff.

Exactly two years after the big eruption, a plume of steam can be seen rising from the dome growing inside the crater of Mount St. Helens.

FIVE

Volcanoes and Life

One day, a hundred years from now, a new forest will be growing on the north slope of Mount St. Helens. Everything that lived on the slope before May 18, 1980, will be able to live there again. For the earth is a planet of life, and volcanoes are part of the earth. Volcanoes destroy some life when they erupt, but they also help to make life possible.

The earth has many volcanoes. Some are dead, or extinct, and will never erupt again. Some are active, giving off lava and gases. Many are sleeping, or dormant. They are quiet now, but at some time they will erupt again.

Some of these volcanoes are on the ocean floor. Others are on land. Most of the land volcanoes circle the Pacific Ocean. They run from South America to Alaska to Japan, Indonesia, and New Zealand. Together they are known as the Ring of Fire. Nearly all the other land volcanoes are in a belt that runs from Indonesia to the Mediterranean Sea.

For many years this belt and the Ring of Fire were a scientific puzzle. Why were most land volcanoes in these two regions? Today earth scientists think they know the answer. It has to do with movements of the earth's crust.

The crust is a shell of solid rock. We live on the crust, but we do not see much of it. Most of it is covered with soil and oceans. Beneath the

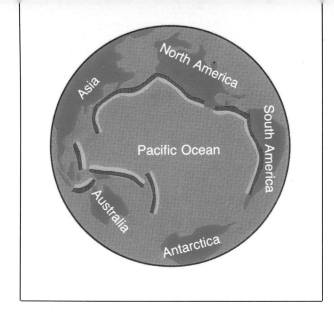

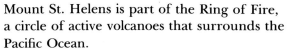

Mount St. Helens is part of the Ring of Fire, a circle of active volcanoes that surrounds the Pacific Ocean.

crust is a region called the mantle. It is made of rock that is very hot. Rock of the mantle can flow, like thick tar. The crust floats on the mantle.

Earth scientists used to think that the crust was all one piece, like the shell of an egg. Now they think it is broken into a number of huge slabs, which they call plates. Each plate is made up of rock of the crust and rock of the upper mantle.

The plates are in motion, moving a few inches each year. The movement is something like that of the belt in a checkout counter. The belt rises in one place. It moves along, carrying whatever is on top of it. It turns down in another place. As the plates move, they too carry whatever is on top of them—the ocean floor, islands, and whole continents.

There are places where plates pull away from each other. Here molten rock wells up and sometimes volcanoes erupt. Over hundreds of thousands of years, the molten rock has built a ridge. The ridge runs through the earth's oceans, all around the globe, like the seam on a baseball. At this mid-ocean ridge new material is added to plates that are moving apart. It is like the place where the checkout belt comes up.

There are also places where plates collide. Here one plate turns down, as the belt does, and slides under the other into the mantle. Here rock melts, magma rises, and volcanoes may erupt. That is what happens all around the rim of the Pacific Ocean.

In the Pacific Northwest, a small ocean plate is colliding with the big plate carrying North America. The small plate slides under the big one.

52

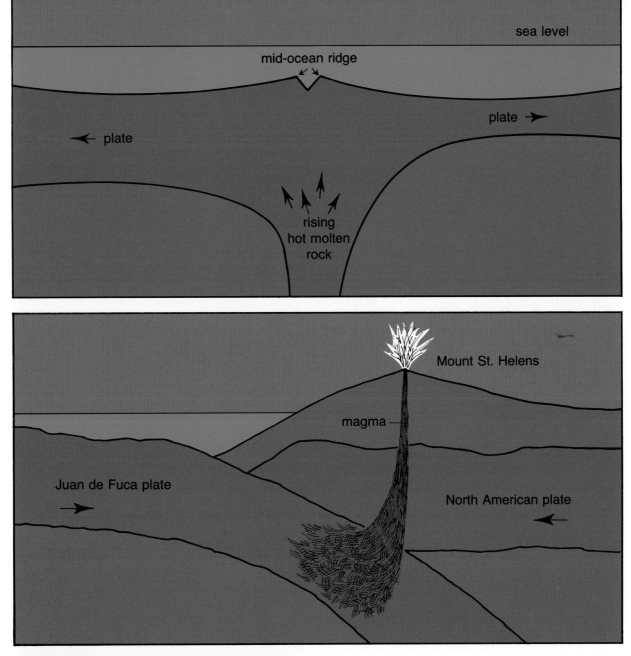

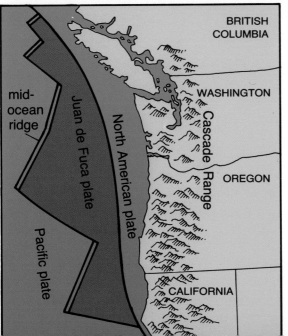

Top: The mid-ocean ridge is where plates move apart. Here molten rock wells up from inside the earth and is added to the trailing edges of the plates.

Center: Where plates collide, one turns down and slides under the other into the mantle. Here rock melts, magma rises, and volcanoes may erupt.

Left: In the Pacific Northwest, the small Juan de Fuca plate is moving eastward from the mid-ocean ridge. It collides with the big plate carrying North America. The small plate slides under the big one. Here eruptions have built the Cascade Range.

Mosses and other low-growing plants now cover the slope behind the mountain ash. They will serve as seedbeds for other plants as life returns.

Here eruptions have built the Cascade Range. Here volcanoes, such as Mount St. Helens, still erupt from time to time.

A big eruption seems like a disaster to us, especially if lives are lost. But volcanoes also help to make the earth a planet of life.

Volcanic eruptions add gases to the atmosphere and water to the oceans. Some earth scientists think that when the earth was very young, eruptions may have given our planet its first atmosphere and oceans.

Volcanoes are builders of land. Floods of lava have built big chunks of continents, such as the Columbia Plateau in the Pacific Northwest. Volcanoes build some of the earth's mountains and some of its islands. They make places where people, animals, and plants can exist.

Volcanoes are also makers of soil. Ash, pumice, and other forms of lava break down in time. They mix with the remains of plants and animals, making a rich soil. The soil nourishes plants, which support many other forms of life.

Volcanoes destroy, but they also build. And after each eruption life does come back, finding small footholds and spreading.

Natural scientists knew that life would return to the north side of Mount St. Helens. But they were awed by how quickly it came back, by its ability to survive, by the way it appeared in even the most unlikely places.

One group of scientists found insects and seeds on a dome rock.

One natural scientist visited the crater after the explosive eruptions stopped. At first he felt he was on another planet. He was standing in a rocky bowl with sides that rose 2,000 feet above his head. Rock falls kept rumbling down them. Clouds of gases and ash rose from vents in the lava dome. Near him was a rock the size of a small house.

The rock, which had erupted from inside the mountain, was a new part of the earth's surface. A greenish patch caught the scientist's eye. He found that algae, simple green plants, were already growing on the rock. He began to walk around it, looking for life. He saw a ladybug with 11 spots, starting to move around as the sun warmed it. He found a wasp laying eggs on the rock. He found flies everywhere. Then he came on a different kind of ladybug, with only two spots. He found a moth that was the same color as the rock. Finally he discovered a little opening in the rock where a bird had spent some time, perhaps an evening—there were its droppings, which contained the remains of insects. "All this life," the scientist said in wonder, "on just one rock."

The naturalist saw a rock the size of a small house.

On the rock he saw many kinds of life, including algae, ladybugs, and flies.

That life, like the islands of life and the silver clouds of seeds and insects, was a promise. It was a promise of the time when all St. Helens would once more be a green and pleasant mountain and home to many, many kinds of animals and plants.

Index